Woodfire, Smoke, and Broken Things

Eileen Burnett

BookLeaf Publishing

India | USA | UK

Presentation by *BookLeaf Publishing*

Web: www.bookleafpub.com

E-mail: info@bookleafpub.com

ISBN: 9789358318609

First edition 2024

For everyone who still lives to overcome,

despite the pain.

You are not alone.

ACKNOWLEDGEMENT

There are so many people for whom a great deal of gratitude is deserved.

My parents, for never giving up on me. For believing in me to the point of utter sacrifice, which is the very definition of love. Your love and support were, at times, the only reason I lived. The only reason I went on. Your love for me is the reason I was able to write this today.

My children, for enduring the hardship that was my healing, and loving me anyway. You are a gift. A treasure. I didn't deserve you, but you thrived in spite of me. I am so proud of you, my sons.

My best friend, who encourages me in all the ways that only the rarest of true friends do. In you I found sisterhood. In you I found strength. In you is a soul worth knowing.

My professors at the Humanities Department at UHCL. You have no idea what it took for me to be there every day. To push past the tears, to break through the chains, and learn to speak for myself. But you saw. Every day, year after year, you mentored me. In your eyes I saw who I could be. I saw compassion and hope. I will always be grateful for your patience as I learned to speak, your guidance as I learned to stand, and your encouragement as I learned to fly.

And to my Heavenly Father, who, through the work of the Holy Spirit, gave me beauty for ashes.

PREFACE

Poetry has always been in my blood.

It's how I see the world, from the slow and careful dance of the caterpillar spinning its chrysalis, to the evening procession of birds flowing like a river in the sky.

To me, poetry is life, and in that life, pains and struggles have purpose, creating a resilience of character that is as fiercely beautiful as it is necessary. It is why the most awe-inspiring things in this life draw us; the mountains, the oceans, the forest... all their majesty is amplified by the harshest of conditions in which they thrive.

This particular collection of poetry is birthed from that place of intersection. The place where pain meets determination. Where strength is found in the most unlikely of places. Where echoes of loves lost still haunt our dreams, and where the lonely road that goes on forever takes on the mantle of adventure.

Walk with me, just for a little while...

Broken Things

How strange a time in which we live
When fauna's life means more than his.
We sympathize with beaten dog
Yet treat mankind much worse than hog,
Recognizing signs o'misuse
Which culminate in harsh abuse
That leads the beast in actions to
Be fearful, meek, and violent too.

We bend and teeter, cave and switch
A harrowed eye, compassion's kiss
And dutifully spend the days
Recalculating misdeed's ways,
Justifying actions bad
For sad reaction to what they had.

Yet brother, sister, neighbor sway
In such like manner, come what may-
The fury of indignance leashed
Gives rise to wrath upon his seat,
Ostracizing friend and foe
For displaying natural weakness so,
As though the blows to soul and mind
Could be repaired with cheese and wine
And laughter, to ignore the scars

Of harsh neglect, abuse, and wars
Fought for the soul, to remain alive-
The depths to which one's spirit dives,
Immeasurable, yet no credit given
For finding reason to go on living...

For broken things are only loved
If tail and fur make soft a hug.

Seven

Blinded by the flash of blue
I fell into the arms of you
Who told me what I'd yearned to hear
A torch you held for 13 years
What's wrong?
And daughter, too, she loved me so
For books and laughter, as mem'ry goes
Impact the very best of us
To see what time has really lost
It's nothing, really.
But fear can raise its ugly head
Tearing, gnashing, burning red
Within the hearts of undealt pain
Restricting love's unworthy bane
Just tell me.
Reducing open river flow
To trickle then repellant sew
In binding stich Love's loss unseen
The searing pain came back again
Please.
Burrowed itself so deep inside
To pull away, to run, to hide
To seek escape from exposed mess
Rejected with such carelessness
I hid.

For seven years I've spent in grief
Learned it was only self-deceit
To keep you in my heart so low
I think it's time to let you go.
I live.

Fijate (Listen)

Walking down the hallway
Uncertainty abounds
The heaviness of my footsteps
Echoing
A little too loud for my taste,
A little too proud for my race-
So I breathe and step lightly
Cursing the shoes for their betrayal
Reminding me of the burden of failure that
Sticks to my thighs like glue
A jiggling, visual reminder of
What dreams never came.

Fijate, these shoes,
they didn't make this noise when I tried them on,
Those gems of the back clearance isle,
Calling out to me
That I didn't have to stay frumpy,
-Vestido como una vieja!-
That I could choose something youthful,
Just for me,
Something to remind me of
The woman I used to be
The woman I want to be
The woman I still could be...

And not feel guilty about it.

There was no one there to tell me I couldn't
No one there to berate me, or
Show up to remove me
From a place where I was told
I didn't belong.
My head, spinning at the decisions,
Echoes of
"You are a nobody!" and
"You don't even know what you want!"
Buzz like gnats on ripe fruit, and I
Sink down into the chair
To catch my breath.

I sit, for what seems to be hours,
Contemplating the reasons I can buy myself
Those shoes
Canceling out the feelings that
Negate my right
To just peruse
Or buy even,
If I so choose
For me.

So, I swat those flies away, and
Say to myself
Soy yo!
Me gustan!

Soy libre!!!
And suddenly the room erupts with
Trumpets and drums,
Celia Cruz on the stage, shaking her
Thickness
With all the confidence of her generations.
"Soy El savor tropical" bursts through my mind,
And suddenly, I am
Walking with her,
up to the front,
buzzing gnats gone
Replaced with a
Fire
Whose embers longed to revive.

So I bought those shoes,
and wore them,
the klop-klopping of the heels, now a
bittersweet victory for my ego.
I walked and winced at the noise,
tempted to curse them again...
but stopped myself,
remembering those drums.
I love these shoes, I think to myself.
I need these shoes, I plead with myself.
I deserve these shoes, I reminded myself,
to go with the hand-me-down
ropa que me han regalado,
las mujeres de la Iglesia que pensaron que yo era

un "charity case",
la mujer sin esposo,
without resources, y
sin remedio.

"La pobre" they would whisper, as their eyes
reflected
pity
judgment, and
ignorance
as to why I was there,
their own shoes click clinking with their
little dainty feet on their
Little dainty legs
that held no burdens at all.

They thought it was their Jesus, but
really,
it was their
rich ass husbands and their
uncomplicated lives
that led to such easy smiles.
It's not hard to be happy when you have no lack.
So I accepted their clothes
put on their jewelry
and masked my race with a smile.

I am careful in my walking now.
I make it to the room,

y ese hombre, me mira,
he looks at my shoes
but I am dancing in my mind.
ready to be heard
ready to matter
-sin verguenza- and
despite my fears.

I look around,
those young faces bereft of pain
showing only exhaustion for the workload
that we all signed up for
the workload that promises
an easier indentured servitude
if we see it to the end.
Conversations of culture,
of class,
of countless other things that make my heart
swell for ideas
these thoughts are a delicacy for me
I eat my fill.

But then he, ese punietero hombre,
turns,
looking at my shoes,
at the ease of my smile, and he
ridicules me
in front of all
calling out my privilege

and I stop
to take it all in.
I try to move the arm back, to
remarry the phonograph needle with her mate,
but it's no use.
The music stops,
the drums go quiet, and
the buzzing gnats appear once again.

A second time he calls me out,
and through the buzzing cloud I hear
a reminder of how
I am the oppressor, with
no understanding of culture,
an ignorant plebeian
negating the hard work of the real laborers
with my impromptu feast of
pickles, berries, and hummus.

I think for a moment,
my ears hot with embarrassment
and I am ashamed.

But why?
Cociendo ropa porque no habia dinero
and I am privileged?
Comiendo arroz con frijoles negros cada dia
and I am privileged?
Years spent watching others eat Cheetos

And Little Debbies
Bacon and cookies, or
Going to MacDonald's while I had a packed
lunch of
sandwiches and water,
My treats were never pies or cakes, but
dulce de guayaba
with a bit of cheese
one head of lettuce for a family of 5
powdered milk and ramen, and
I am privileged?

I look at him, and
try not to cry.

Frozen, I couldn't speak, that
puñetero hombre que no sabia nada,
Thinking he knew me
because of a mask I never learned to shed?

Who does he think he is?

Fijate, ese hombre,
he lived in a different world,
one where it was normal
to speak to a woman as though
she doesn't know pain
because of the lightness in my step,
the twinkle in my eye, and

the drums that beat in my heart.
He couldn't hear the music over
his own ego, ese
punietero hombre
que no podia ver.
He couldn't see, or
wouldn't see
this woman
trying to pick herself up,
empesar una vida,
separarse del martillo,
the hammer,
que le han dado,
Aplastando todo sus suenos
su espiritu
su alma
Con palabras que...
With words so thoughtless they maimed.

And so, here you are
looking at me.
Here, you smirk at me
at my shoes,
at my life,
at the beating drum of my heart that had
found those beautiful black grooves once again,
violently swatting away the gnats
but for the promise of a future.
It is time.

I gather my things, and
carefully remind myself of
who I am,
cranking the handle until the trumpets sound
their melodies once again.
Gnats may be attracted to ripe fruit,
Pero el viento que me cuida, me hace libre,
Keeping them from hovering too long.

I distribute the leftovers, and
walk back down the hallway,
not bothering to stifle the sound.

El ritmo de la vida is mine.
My privilege is coming here.

Fíjate, hombre.
These shoes cost more than you know.

Taking Flight

Last night the house
shifted
breathed out a last breath of that
unique essence that was
you.
It held it for a bit,
trying to taste that part of
you
that had just said goodbye with
a cheerful see ya
not knowing what was to be.

The house held it
a little bit longer
as if it could hold time in suspension
in utero
in breath
and you would never leave.

I felt it
holding
just for a while,
as I made my way to sleep,
locking the doors
setting the bars down, and

nestling myself
between the sheets and oblivion...

And there it was!
The great exhale,
one so terrible and mighty
that it sent tears from the sky
and my eyes,
that releasing of a presence that was
as much a part of it
as the dogs,
those sentinels of the night,
or the bookshelves, those
atlases of hopes and dreams
Too fanciful for a single lifetime.

I didn't want it to be
but, there it was,
a sudden gasp for
something
no longer there,
and I lay there
eyes open
feeling the vacuum
filling in now with
the rush of
all that remains
of me.

Sway

This tightrope that I'm walking
-without an inch to spare-
it hovers over the abyss
suspended in midair.
It bends and sways with changes
from the valleys of despair,
it threatens death with every step;
the path, its only care

Its purpose is direction,
to lead and guide the way.
It cares not for my comfort or
if I have fallen prey
to fears and such anxieties
presented, as I stay
my course, balanced on a thread of
truth. I cry and then I pray.

It terrifies and thrills me
because of where I go:
From mountaintop to mountaintop,
avoiding common roads
and the pitfalls that are on them-
those hazards weigh like stones;
for on each path, they're no longer mine,

While rope remains my home.

I must keep focus now.
To sway is danger, to fall
is death. But while I sway, my hand
is held, my heart recalls
the One who has me, through
this journey. Baggage lost

Means nothing.

Sonnet 1- The Journey

Alone in a sea of people, we are wayfarers,
sailing with no compass, and no ground
from which we can but gain our bearings. Far
away there is a call, and it resounds
against the sonorous cavern of our hearts,
reverberations pricking insecurity,
goading us to seek, to want, to find
some peaceful respite from this arduous journey.
Above, the guyed mast is true and straight,
a technological Etruscan wonder from
which to place our trust in. Our fate
has not yet come to pass. Ho! Look! The sun
has peeked out from the shrouded mist, and now
we see, and know, and become this journey's
plough.

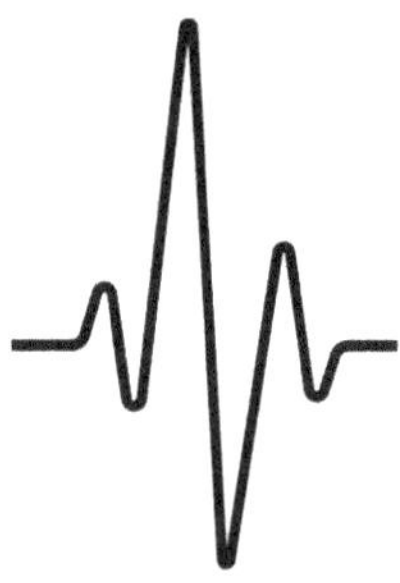

Breath

The air tonight has a bite to it
Like from gunpowder
or fireworks
This November evening's mantle
Thick with dew
It lingers.
Where it came from
I don't know
In this soggy mess
One can only
Speculate
As the stars
Refuse
To answer.
They hide
In fear, or shame,
For what is soon to come
Rain like tears
Falling
Lamenting the loss
Of love's
Quiet rest.
Where will you go
When myth becomes real
When fountains erupt

With the wrath of the deep?
The bite of the air
Will dig into your flesh
And all eyes will open
To light

The Hour

Looking out my window
I see them in the air
A thousand little flying things
All buzzing without a care
They glide with boundless wings of grace,
Of carelessness and joy
All singing an unceasing tune
To every girl and boy
Who would to turn their head to look
And hear rather than cacophony
A choir of seabirds flying overhead
All headed home with glee
Looking out my window
I see them in the air
One of my favorites of day
To this I stop and stare
For few things capture wonder
Like the joyous flying birds
Set flight against an evening sky
Too beautiful for words
And so I stop and marvel
At these beauties every day
It is my favorite thing to do
My favorite time of day

The Ritual

Night is falling!
Oh, can you see
Orion and his mighty bow?
Directly overhead,
by the moon's ardent pulse,
he is aiming at her, crouched within
the tree of solace.

She stands sentry,
her glow illuminating all,
aware of his presence, yet
unperturbed
for who can extinguish her light?
Many have tried, and yet she remains, still,
unusually positioned for this
strange thing to come.

Below, two women
howl in glee around a fire of
sticks and stones laid waste by
years
tears
and the wisdom of letting go.
Flames join their dance as the drums beat,
anticipating climax.

Later, they shiver by the cynthian light,
shiver in the knowing that
this central presence in the heavens
marked a changing of the times
a changing of the guard
an ushering in of a new season for which
their ill equipped wardrobes
resonated.

They huddled, and watched him,
frozen in his hunter's stance
of victory over the light.

Son of the sea, why do you rage
against that which moves
your blood?
Do you not know your efforts are in vain
oh giant of the night sky?

Tickle

Sunlight
Peeking over the
horizon,
anticipating the coming caresses
the promise of a new day.
Beams build, lapping over one another,
each charged electron racing a
million miles an hour in
eagerness
of what's to come,
beckoned by the force of a thousand caresses
she moves
propelled by might
ignited by the tickle on the nape of her neck,
breath, shallow and hot,
pulsating with the
ferocity of a shudder.
Particles leap with the excitement of a
newly kindled furnace
hot and steady,
reaching across the sky
with fingers that respond to the
immersion,
Liquid azure pools of love.
She wakes
and sees herself as once again
alive.

The Empty Room

Sleep whispers my name
bidding me come
out from the day and its sorrows,
away from the memories of you
into the world of pillows
of dreams
into a land of possibility,
and my eyes grow heavy.
Sleep calls through the empty room
and I obey,
head lolling as I
find my way to my pillow with ease.
Sleep wraps its arms around me
and in the twilight
-that liminal space where spirits walk-
you come to me.

Room filled now
your presence unmistakable and powerful.
You stand
watching
eyes lingering on my
body
sprawled casually among the pillows.
For a moment you hesitate

then
a knee touches my bed
then a hand
then another
and I feel the charged atmosphere
as your body hovers over mine,
longing
whispering
pleading
your breath tickling my neck
as words with no sound
caress my heart.
Startled, I open my eyes
searching for a figure
whose echo still resounds
in the space between us,
but all I find is an empty room,
a tear-stained pillow,
and the warmth of my skin
where your spirit
touched mine.

Joy

Joy is a nest full of
beaks open wide
hidden between branches
of an old olive tree.
For mother and father
they tirelessly work
preparing their little ones
for the day they fly free.

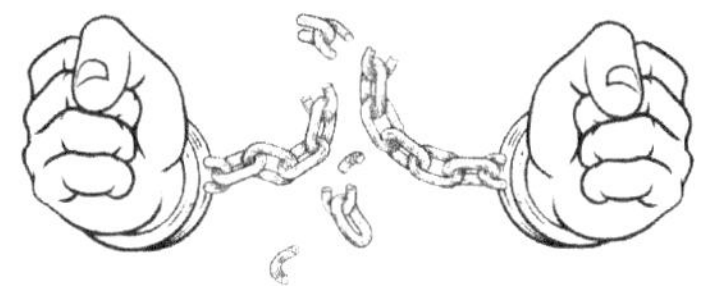

Ghost

I see it now.
I get it.

There was never any part of me that you loved.
Never any part of me that you cherished
Adored
Held dear for any other reason than
the covetous looks you enjoyed
the free labor I provided
And the nights you took as your right,
Regardless of how I felt.

I see it now.
I get it.

That part of me that was ME,
that part that should have enraptured you
drawn you
spurred you to become better,
encouraged you in all your endeavors,
lifting us both to a higher place
whose limitations were only the ones WE
chose...
That part of me...
the part that was ME

would never be enough.
For every victory I had
only served as a reminder of your failures,
an arrow of accusation
from which you could never escape.

I see it now.
I get it.

My strength reminded you of your weakness
My vibrancy of your dullness
My intelligence of your lack
and there was nothing I could ever do for that.
No,
not for that.

For you were not interested in growth
or companionship
or adventure, but in
moulding in me a receptacle for your
inadequacies
carving out a doll from your phylacteries
from which to
puppet out your bullshit
rebranded with a smile.

I see it now.
I get it.

For this I lived as a widow,
haunted by the ghost of a man
who never was
shackled to a body with no memory of a mouth,
and
sentenced for crimes transferred to me
by way of the smoke in the mirror.
I raised children in secret.
Learned how to be less
so that you could always feel more,
protecting your dignity with words like
I'm sorry and
It's okay, and
It's my fault...
Lies that only made you hate yourself more
because the ghost in you knew
the truth

But no more.

I see it now.
I get it.

There is nothing in me that can
ever satisfy
the emptiness in you.
Nothing that can make you change.
No love is enough
no forgiveness too great

to satiate
your hatred for life
for people
for me, and
the youth I stole from you.

There is nothing in me that ever should be
that which you should be doing yourself.

What was done for you
you reject,
and so I dust off my shoes
and say...

Goodbye.

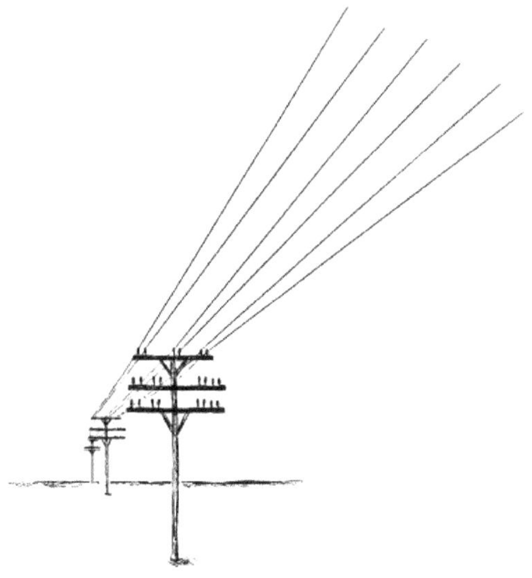

Flags

45

When will liberation come
With its sound of solace
Second only
To another helping of lamb stew?
You don't know what it is
To sit in a city
Ripe with tension
And jump to the streetlights
Suddenly
For a hope
Delivered
By wire.
So sit with me
Beside the lightbox
Gleaming with lives past
We will have a glass of red
Ripe with glory
And talk about
Tomorrow.

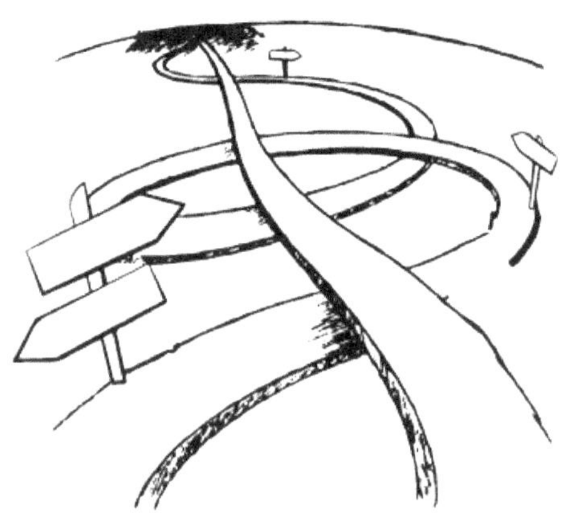

The Battle

The clashing of the seasons
The changing of the tides
The war it rages on and on
We take it all in strides
We see it coming miles away
We're ready for the fight
Yet still it caught us all off guard
Regardless of our might
For no one thinks it to be here
We'll live another day
In blissful sleepy ignorance
We go about our way
Flapping gums and gnashing teeth
Those marionetting fakes
And yet the battle rages on
It trembles and it quakes
The ground beneath our very feet
As we look the other way
As buildings fall and regimes do crumble
And suddenly our voices mute
Will most of us remain too silent
Till all our rights they are refused
To those who live to see the dawn
Of this so dreadful day
The battle rages on and on
For those who see the way

Them

Azure eyes,
blinded by the
seafoam spray off the ship
He takes his drug store glasses, and
rubs the snowy white clouds from the sky.

And then he sees her
golden as she walks,

she shines with brilliance
tongue tingling
the copper taste
drew him to his knees
siphoning ego from his breast.

Their spirits meet
ephemeral rainbows
traversing down emerald slopes
that amber melting into pools of
liquid calamity.

The Ballad of the Squirrels, Part One

We chase them off, and now they wait
a mariachi band of squirrels
all sitting in a three-tiered state
awaiting some of nature's pearls.
They chitter to the passers-by
in flight, on wheel, on foot,
they chitter madnesses and cry
an anthem that forsook
all others, for their vengeances,
so awful towards us now,
for barring those sweet nuts and treats
that cycle with their plough.
They look, and wait for openings
(for humans oft retreat
to silly things, like looking at
little boxes while they eat.)
They searched for ways to reach the box
where said delicacies lie,
To El Dorado! was the hymn
that they were heard to cry.
But sadly, there was no resolve
no spoils to mark the day,
for guarding entrance to the door
was the mighty man, the jay.

This is What Healing Looks Like

In the morning, I listen
patiently waiting for that time
that feeling
that moment when the fullness of nature and her
majesty
-that stillness in the breeze that calls
my innermost being
out of the chaos and
into the light-
stirs my soul.

I wait, and breathe,
the solitude a simple pleasure, yet something in
it
calls me to
warm smiles,
whipped icing on cake, and
the strum of a guitar chord
played against the backdrop of stars.
I smile and breathe in the promise.

In the evening,
the flames, they
lick the sky

caress the wind
and radiate a presence that is
reflected in the eyes of my friends
the boughs of the trees, and the
laughter that suddenly bursts out
uniting us in spirit
and song.

Woodfire and Smoke

The air is still
pierced occasionally by the trilling calls of
sandhill cranes crying out to the wind, the
shudder of horses, and
the dying breath of the season's last flowers.
It is peaceful.
Bees drone in the sunshine with the urgency of
hunger
as the temperature begins to drop
signaling the weary to rest
the sleeping to prey, and those who remain to
their
woodfires and smoke.

Later, the landscape changes.
A hush settles on the horizon,
anticipation of the prairie wolf's hunt,
stealthy markers of the agency of the wild.
A scream.
Another resident of Nihm is lost to the great
horned owl,
and rabbits shiver in their dens,
and kiss their children goodnight.

Hidden in their boxes of ones and zeros,

man sees nothing but his own folly.
A few venture out, roaring in their hubris,
drowning the night's sounds in bourbon and
metal,
pits dimming perceptions.
Flames lick the sky
as the moon watches
patient in her vigil
guarding them all with her light.

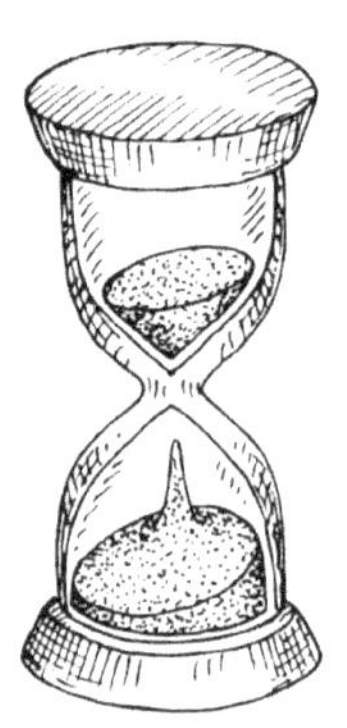

The Beard of Sorrow

He walked with a hunchback
His beard was square
He nodded as he spoke to the air
His legs they would wobble
With the weight of a failure
That riddled his mind and
Stripped life of the dignity
That he had inherited so long ago

The beard of sorrow
It passes through lifetimes
Trying to find its way home
It drifts in the wind where
Somebody out there
Moves just to let the man through

But it's only the smell of
A lifetime of failures
Of hope that had festered to gray
Nobody noticed
He only just passed them
He's already forgotten today

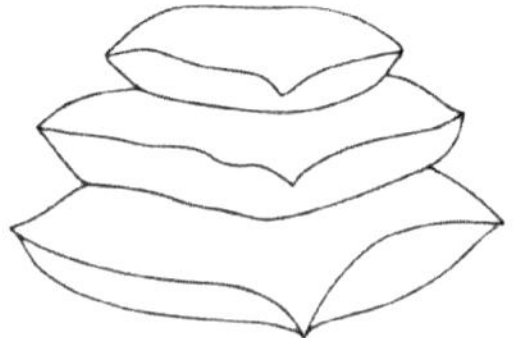

Pillows

There are too many pillows on the top of my old
bed
But each one has a memory lingering round my
weary head
I hold on to each and every one cause I cannot
let them go
It's the smell of you my sweet love, and your
promises they hold.
There's the one we took out camping
Where the flicker in your eyes reflected all
God's Majesty
You asked me why I cried
But my heart was just so full with you that you
took me in your arms
We really never left that tent, and the pillow held
our hearts.

There's another, smells of roses (those are the
ones you brought me, Dear,
that time you surprised my heavy heart and
quenched my every fear)
You laid me down so sweetly on that pillow
lined with red
Whose sweetly fragrant petals still send ripples
through my head.

Then there's the one from Phoenix, from that
road trip in your car
Or the one we brought from your old ranch, the
one with yellow stars
That pillowcase is faded now, but it still smells
fresh as rain
Reminding me that times with you I'm always
safe from pain.

So I know that there's a lot of them
Too many some would say
But each and every one has got a story in its own
way
The softest dreams of lovers and transitions that
we do
Through life's amazing chapters that I get to do
with you

So how can I just throw away that pillow laced
with tears
Or the one that propped our baby up, or this one,
bought last year,
It just started fitting my head right- you know
that's hard to do-
So you tell me to make a decision, but they all
just point to you,
Cause each and every pillow Is a piece of me
and you

There are too many pillows on the top of my old
bed
But each one has a memory lingering round my
weary head
I hold on to each and every one because I cannot
let them go
It's the smell of you my sweet love and your
promises they hold
It's the smell of you my sweet love and your
promises they hold